ABOUT THE AUTHOR

Neil Ardley has written a number of innovative nonfiction books for children, including *The Eyewitness Guide to Music*. He also worked closely with David Macaulay on *The Way Things Work*. In addition to being a well-known author in the fields of science, technology, and music, he is an accomplished musician who composes and performs both jazz and electronic music. He lives in Derbyshire, England, with his wife and daughter.

Project Editors Scott Steedman and Laura Buller
Art Editors Mark Regardsoe and Earl Neish
Production Louise Barratt
Photography Dave King
Created by Dorling Kindersley Limited, London

Library of Congress Cataloging-in-Publication Data
Ardley, Neil.
The science book of energy/Neil Ardley.—1st U.S. ed.
p. cm.
"Gulliver books."
Summary: Gives instructions for a variety of simple experiments that explore and explain different forms of energy.
ISBN 0-15-200611-7
1. Force and energy—Experiments—Juvenile literature.
[1. Force and energy—Experiments. 2. Experiments.] I. Title.
QC73.4.A75 1992
531'.6—dc20 91-18094

Printed in Belgium by Proost
First U.S. edition 1992
A B C D E

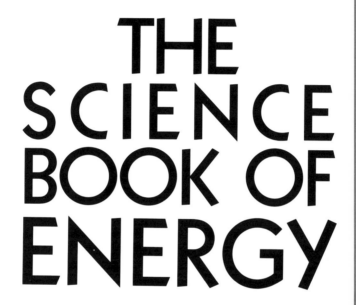

THE SCIENCE BOOK OF ENERGY

Neil Ardley

HBJ

Gulliver Books

Harcourt Brace Jovanovich, Publishers

San Diego   New York   London

What is energy?

Making anything move or change—walking across a street, boiling water, or powering a machine—takes energy. Energy is what makes things happen. Most energy comes from the sun in the forms of heat and light. Sound, electricity, and movement are also types of energy.

Striking oil!
The oil from this refinery can be burned to make energy. We use such fuels as oil, coal, and gas to heat our homes, schools, and offices.

Catching some rays
On a sunny day, you can feel and see the sun's energy. Heat energy makes you feel warm, and light energy makes everything bright.

Making a move
Playing soccer takes a lot of energy. In fact, you use energy every time you move.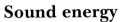

Sound energy
You make energy travel to others when you sing or talk. Sound energy, in the form of vibrations, moves from your throat to other people's ears.

Storing energy
This house is heated by the energy of the sun—even at night. Special panels store the sun's heat during the day for use at night.

⚠ This is a warning symbol. It appears within experiments next to steps that require caution. When you see this symbol, ask an adult for help.

Be a safe scientist
Follow all the instructions carefully and always use caution, especially with glass, scissors, matches, and sharp objects. Cutting thick plastic can be dangerous. When experiments require cutting plastic bottles or making holes, ask an adult. And take care when handling cut edges—they can be very sharp.

Energy for life

Like all animals and plants, you need energy to live. This energy comes originally from the sun in the forms of heat and light. Find out how you are able to take in the sun's energy.

You will need:

Two slices of buttered bread

Glass jar

Disposable dishcloth

Bowl

Tablespoon

Alfalfa seeds

Water

Rubber band

1 Fill the glass jar with water. Pour in a tablespoon of alfalfa seeds and allow them to soak overnight.

2 The next day, cover the top of the jar with the dishcloth. Hold it in place with the rubber band.

Make sure the seeds are completely covered with water.

3 Pour the water out through the dishcloth. Then cover the seeds with fresh water.

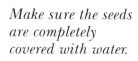

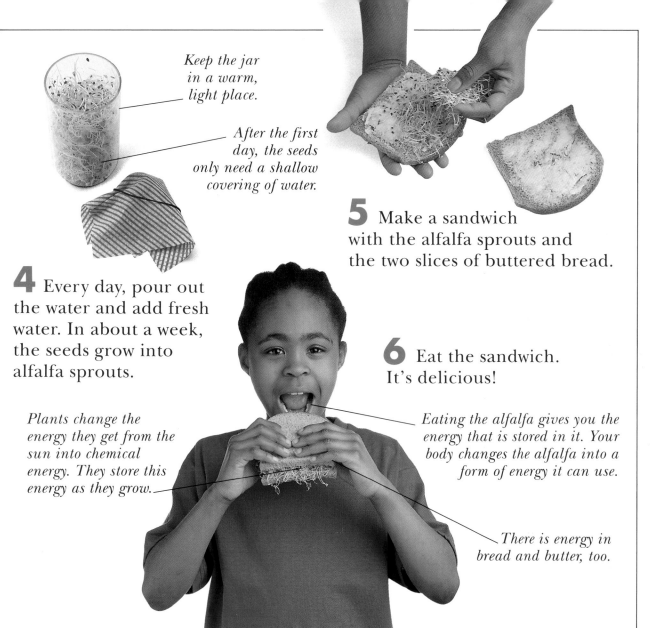

Keep the jar in a warm, light place.

After the first day, the seeds only need a shallow covering of water.

5 Make a sandwich with the alfalfa sprouts and the two slices of buttered bread.

4 Every day, pour out the water and add fresh water. In about a week, the seeds grow into alfalfa sprouts.

6 Eat the sandwich. It's delicious!

Plants change the energy they get from the sun into chemical energy. They store this energy as they grow.

Eating the alfalfa gives you the energy that is stored in it. Your body changes the alfalfa into a form of energy it can use.

There is energy in bread and butter, too.

Body building

Eating food, such as this corn, gives us the energy we need to grow, build up our bodies, and stay alive. Some foods, such as sugar, contain a lot of energy. If we take in more energy than we need, our bodies store it as fat, and we may become overweight.

Energy in the air

Motion is a form of energy called "kinetic energy." By building a pinwheel you can make use of the kinetic energy of moving air just as a windmill does.

You will need:

Square of stiff paper

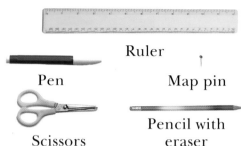
Ruler

Pen

Map pin

Scissors

Pencil with eraser

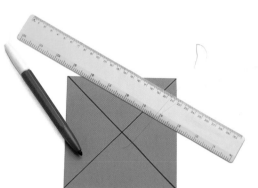

1 Draw two diagonal lines on the square of paper.

Poke the holes on the same side of each line.

2 Make a pinhole beside the line in each corner.

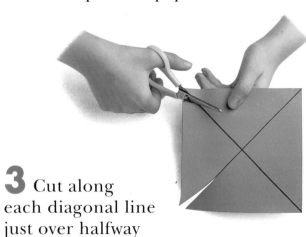

3 Cut along each diagonal line just over halfway to the center of the square.

4 Fold the four corners that have pinholes into the center.

5 ⚠ Push the map pin through the holes and the center of the square. Then push the pin into the side of the pencil's eraser. This is your pinwheel.

The kinetic energy of the moving air is transferred to the pinwheel, making the blades turn.

6 Blow on the pinwheel. The blades spin rapidly.

Power from the wind
These modern windmills change the wind's motion into electricity. Each windmill has an electric generator that converts the kinetic energy of the spinning vanes into electrical energy.

Jumping coin

Can you make a coin jump up and down using only the heat of your hands? See how heat, which is a form of energy, can change into kinetic energy.

You will need:

Quarter

Dish of water

Glass bottle

1 Put the bottle in a refrigerator for about 15 minutes. Then dip the mouth in the water.

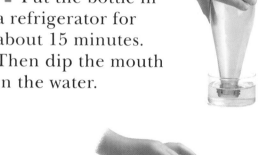

As it warms, the air expands and escapes from the bottle, lifting the coin as it goes.

The heat of your hands warms the air in the bottle.

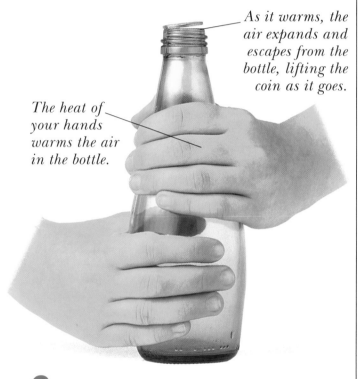

2 Dip the coin in the water. Then put the wet coin on the mouth of the bottle.

3 Place your hands on the sides of the bottle. Hold them still. The coin hops up and down several times!

Gasoline power

This car gets energy from gasoline, which is burned in cylinders in the engine. The heat produced makes air in the cylinders expand, moving parts of the engine and turning the wheels.

Waterwheel

Falling water has lots of kinetic energy. You can build a waterwheel to control and make use of this energy. People once used waterwheels to provide power for many machines.

You will need:

Cork

Modeling clay

Plastic tube

Water

Plastic bottle

Funnel

Tape

Stiff plastic

Glass dish

Nail

Scissors

Two toothpicks

Knife

Space the slits evenly around the cork.

1 ⚠ Ask an adult to make four slits in the side of the cork.

2 Cut four pieces of plastic to the same length as the slits in the cork.

Make sure the plastic blades fit snugly.

3 Slide the plastic blades into the slits in the cork. This is your waterwheel.

4 ⚠ Ask an adult to make two holes on opposite sides of the bottle with the nail.

Continued on next page

5 ⚠ Carefully cut off the bottom of the bottle. Make sure the cut edge is flat enough for the bottle to stand up.

6 ⚠ Push a toothpick into one end of the cork. Put it inside the bottle and push the toothpick through one hole.

The waterwheel should spin easily.

7 ⚠ Put a toothpick through the other hole and push it into the cork. Put clay over the points of the toothpicks.

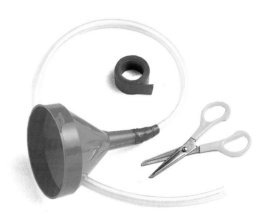

8 Insert the funnel into the plastic tube and tape it in place.

Continued from previous page

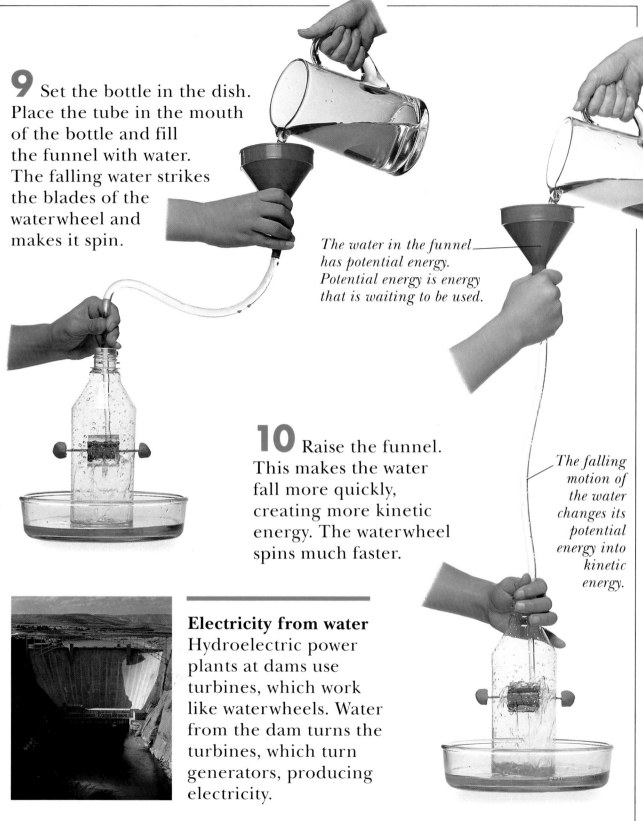

9 Set the bottle in the dish. Place the tube in the mouth of the bottle and fill the funnel with water. The falling water strikes the blades of the waterwheel and makes it spin.

The water in the funnel has potential energy. Potential energy is energy that is waiting to be used.

10 Raise the funnel. This makes the water fall more quickly, creating more kinetic energy. The waterwheel spins much faster.

The falling motion of the water changes its potential energy into kinetic energy.

Electricity from water
Hydroelectric power plants at dams use turbines, which work like waterwheels. Water from the dam turns the turbines, which turn generators, producing electricity.

Reversing roller

Make a rolling toy that returns whenever you try to roll it away. The roller works by storing and then releasing energy.

You will need:

Two used matchsticks

Scissors

Two large metal nuts

Wide plastic jar with lid

Rubber band

Short piece of string

1 Tie the nuts to the rubber band with the string.

Put the holes in the centers of the lid and jar.

2 ⚠ Ask an adult to make small holes in the lid and the base of the jar.

3 Thread the rubber band through the hole in the jar. Insert a matchstick to hold it in place.

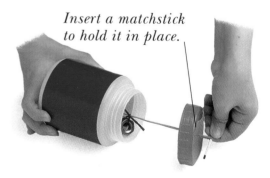

Insert a matchstick to hold it in place.

4 Push the other end of the rubber band through the hole in the lid.

5 Put the lid back on the jar. Make sure it is tight.

As the band unwinds, its potential energy changes back into kinetic energy, making the jar roll backward.

The rolling jar's kinetic energy changes to potential energy in the wound-up rubber band.

6 Roll the jar across the floor. As it rolls forward, the rubber band winds up.

7 The jar comes to a stop. The rubber band unwinds and the jar rolls back to you.

Ready for flight
Stretching back a bow stores potential energy in the bowstring. When the string is released, the potential energy changes into kinetic energy and the arrow flies forward.

Build a battery

Make a battery and use it to create sound. A battery changes chemical energy into electrical energy, or electricity. Electricity can then be changed into sound energy.

You will need:

 Two wires

 Six copper pennies

 Tape

 Pen

 Saucer

 Paper towels

 Scissors

 Headphones

Aluminum foil

Warm salt water

Trace around the edge of a penny to draw the circles.

1 Draw and cut out six foil circles and six paper circles.

If you can't find copper pennies, use nickels or silver coins.

2 Tape one wire to a coin and the other wire to a foil circle.

3 Dip a paper circle in the warm salt water.

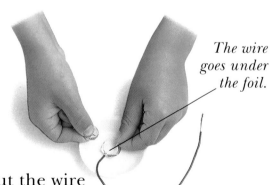

The wire goes under the foil.

4 Put the wire with the foil circle in the saucer. Then put a wet paper circle and a coin on top.

5 Repeat Step 4, building layers of foil, wet paper, and coins. The coin with the wire goes on top. Now you have made a battery.

6 Wrap the end of one wire around the stem of the headphone plug.

Electricity flows from the battery to the headphones. There it is changed into sound energy.

7 Put on the headphones. Scrape the end of the other wire against the tip of the plug. Crackling sounds come from the headphones!

When the aluminum foil, salt, and copper coins are put together, their chemical energy changes into electricity.

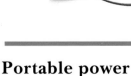

Portable power
Batteries are an energy source you can carry around with you. In this computer game, the electrical energy of the batteries is turned into lights (light energy) and beeps (sound energy).

Flashlight

Build a flashlight and change electricity into light energy. No other form of energy is as easy to use as electricity. It is clean and quiet and works at the flick of a switch.

You will need:

Two C or D cell batteries

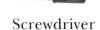
Two paper fasteners

Sharp pencil

Screwdriver

Aluminum foil

Paper clip

Bulb in bulb holder

Cotton

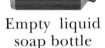
Scissors

Three pieces of wire with bared ends

Tape

Empty liquid soap bottle

Place the holes about 2 cm (1 in.) apart.

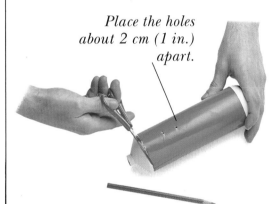

1 ⚠ Ask an adult to cut off the top of the bottle and to make two small holes in the side of the bottle with the pencil.

Place the foil shiny side out.

2 Cover the inside of the bottle top with the foil and tape it in place.

Tape the top of one battery to the bottom of the other.

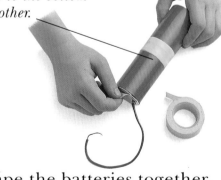

3 Use the screwdriver to attach two pieces of wire to the bulb holder, one to each terminal screw.

4 Tape the batteries together. Tape the third wire to the base of the bottom battery.

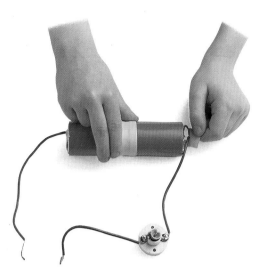

Pack a little cotton around the batteries to hold them in place.

5 Attach one of the wires from the bulb holder to the terminal on the top battery.

6 Thread the loose wire from the bottom battery through the lower hole in the side of the bottle. Slide the batteries into the bottle.

Make sure to remove the bottle cap.

7 Thread the loose wire from the bulb holder through the top hole. Wrap the ends of both wires around the paper fasteners and push the fasteners into the holes in the bottle.

8 Set the bulb holder on top of the batteries and place the bottle top over the bulb. Tape it securely in place.

Continued on next page

9 Bend the paper clip. Then hook one end under the lower paper fastener. This is your switch.

Closing the switch lets electricity flow along the wires from the batteries to the bulb.

10 Press the bent end of the paper clip until it touches the other paper fastener. The bulb lights up!

In the bulb, the electricity changes into light energy.

The light bounces, or reflects, off the foil to produce a beam of light.

Bright lights
Light is a kind of energy known as "radiant" energy because it spreads, or radiates, from its source. A spotlight directs light toward a stage and gives out a lot of light, part of which reflects off the performer. Some of this light then enters our eyes so that we see the person on stage.

Continued from previous page

String sounds

Make sound energy travel along a string and see how energy can travel from one place to another. You communicate by making energy travel to other people.

You will need:

String

Sharp pencil

Fork

Plastic cup

Make a knot in the string to stop it from slipping through the hole.

Hold the cup so that the string is taut.

1 ⚠ Make a small hole in the cup. Thread the string through the hole.

The sound energy travels along the string to the cup.

The prongs vibrate, producing sound energy.

2 Tie the end of the string to the arm of a chair. Hold up the cup. Strike the fork against the edge of a table.

3 Quickly touch the prongs to the lower part of the string. A sound comes from the cup.

Musical strings
You can hear a violin being played because the strings vibrate when they are plucked or stroked with a bow. The vibrations produce sound energy, which travels through the air to your ears.

Energy transfer

Energy cannot be destroyed. When something loses energy, it is either transferred to something else or changed into another kind of energy. See how two fruits transfer energy to one another.

You will need:

Grapefruit

Orange

String

Scissors

1 Cut a piece of string and tie it to the grapefruit, leaving a long, loose end. Do the same with the orange.

Keep this string taut.

Hang the two fruits at the same level.

2 Tie a long piece of string between two fixed points. Suspend both fruits from it.

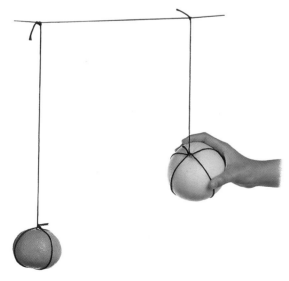

3 Gently pull the grapefruit back and let go. The grapefruit swings back and forth.

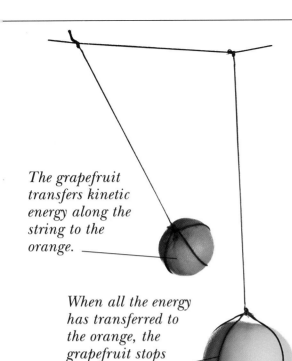

The grapefruit transfers kinetic energy along the string to the orange.

When all the energy has transferred to the orange, the grapefruit stops swinging.

4 When the grapefruit begins to slow down, the orange starts swinging.

The kinetic energy of the orange is transferred back along the string to the grapefruit.

Soon both fruits stop swinging. Their kinetic energy has changed into another kind of energy.

5 When the orange begins to slow down, the grapefruit starts moving again. Each fruit stops and starts a few more times.

Energetic exploits

These circus acrobats are transferring energy to one another. When one acrobat drops onto the seesaw, his kinetic energy is transferred across the board to the other acrobat, who is flung into the air.

Newton's cradle

Can a fixed object suddenly make another object move? Find out by building a toy named after the great scientist Isaac Newton. The toy works because energy cannot be destroyed.

You will need:

Three large beads

Tape

Shoe box

String

Scissors

Modeling clay

String two more beads in the same way.

1 Cut a piece of string. Push one end through the hole in one of the beads. Loop the string around the bead and push it through again.

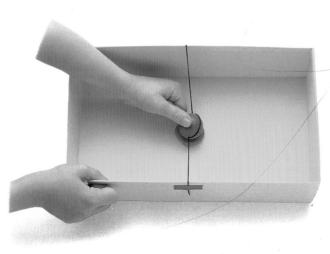

2 Pull the string tight. Lower the bead into the shoe box and pull the string over the opposite edges of the box. Tape it in place.

3 Stick the bead to the base of the box with some clay.

26

4 Lower the other two beads into the box on either side of the fixed bead and tape the strings in place. The beads should just touch the middle bead.

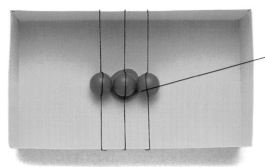

The beads should hang in the center of the box.

The first bead gains kinetic energy as it moves, then transfers this energy to the middle bead when it stops.

5 Pull back the first bead, then let it go. It hits the middle bead and stops. The last bead springs away.

The middle bead cannot move. The kinetic energy is transferred to the last bead and makes it move.

Playing pool

Skillful pool players can make one ball stop as it hits another. When the energy of the first ball transfers to the second, the first stops and the second rolls away.

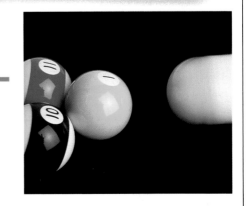

Surface skimmer

Make a boat that skims over a tabletop on a cushion of air. When the air runs out, the skimmer rubs against the table, loses its kinetic energy, and stops.

You will need:

Cork with hole in center

Balloon pump

Paintbrush

Glue

Liquid soap

Stiff cardboard

Clothespin

Pen

Balloon

Scissors

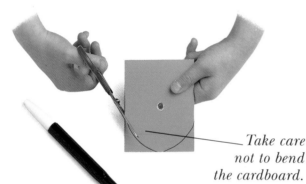

Take care not to bend the cardboard.

1 ⚠ Carefully cut a boat shape from the cardboard. Make a small hole in the center.

2 Firmly glue the cork to the cardboard.

Place the hole in the cork over the hole in the cardboard.

3 Pump up the balloon. Pinch the neck with the clothespin so that no air escapes.

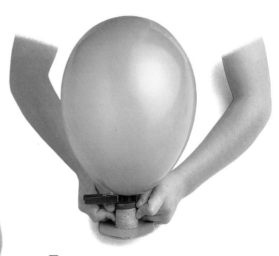

4 Fit the mouth of the balloon over the cork.

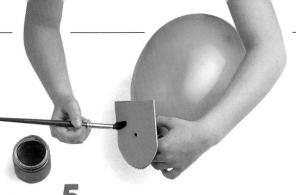

5 Coat the base of the cardboard with liquid soap.

6 Remove the clothespin and push the skimmer. It zooms across the tabletop as the balloon deflates.

The liquid soap reduces the rubbing, or friction, between the skimmer and the tabletop.

Air from the balloon spreads out under the skimmer, lifting it off the tabletop and reducing friction.

Over the waves

A boat uses a lot of energy to push aside the water it moves through. But a hovercraft skims above the water. Air pumped under the hull raises it out of the water, enabling the hovercraft to move more easily.

Picture credits
(Picture credits abbreviation key: B=below, C=center, L=left, R=right, T=top)

Ace Photo Agency: 25BL; Ace Photo Agency/Mugshots: 23BL; Lupe Cuhna Photo Library: 7TR; Zoe Dominic: 22BL; Robert Harding Picture Library: 12BL; The Image Bank/Arthur d'Arazien: 6BL; The Image Bank/Gary Gay: 9BL, 27BR;

The Image Bank/Jane Art Ltd: 17BL; Stockphotos Inc: 15BL; Tony Stone Worldwide: 6T; Zefa Picture Library: 11BL; Zefa Picture Library/H. Schmied: 29BL; Zefa Picture Library/Stockmarket: 7C.

Picture research Kathy Lockley and Clive Webster

Science consultant Jack Challoner

Dorling Kindersley would like to thank Jenny Vaughan for editorial assistance; Mrs Bradbury, Mr Millington, the staff and children of Allfarthing Junior School, Wandsworth, especially Daniel Armstrong, Nadeen Flower, Lucy Gibson, Kemi Owoturo, Casston Rogers-Brown, Ben Sells, Leo Strugnell, Ruth Tross, Kate Ling, and Luke Randall.